Insects Are Animals

CONCEPT SCIENCE

Written by Judith Holloway and Clive Harper
Illustrated by Tim Galloway

Insects have three main parts to their bodies.

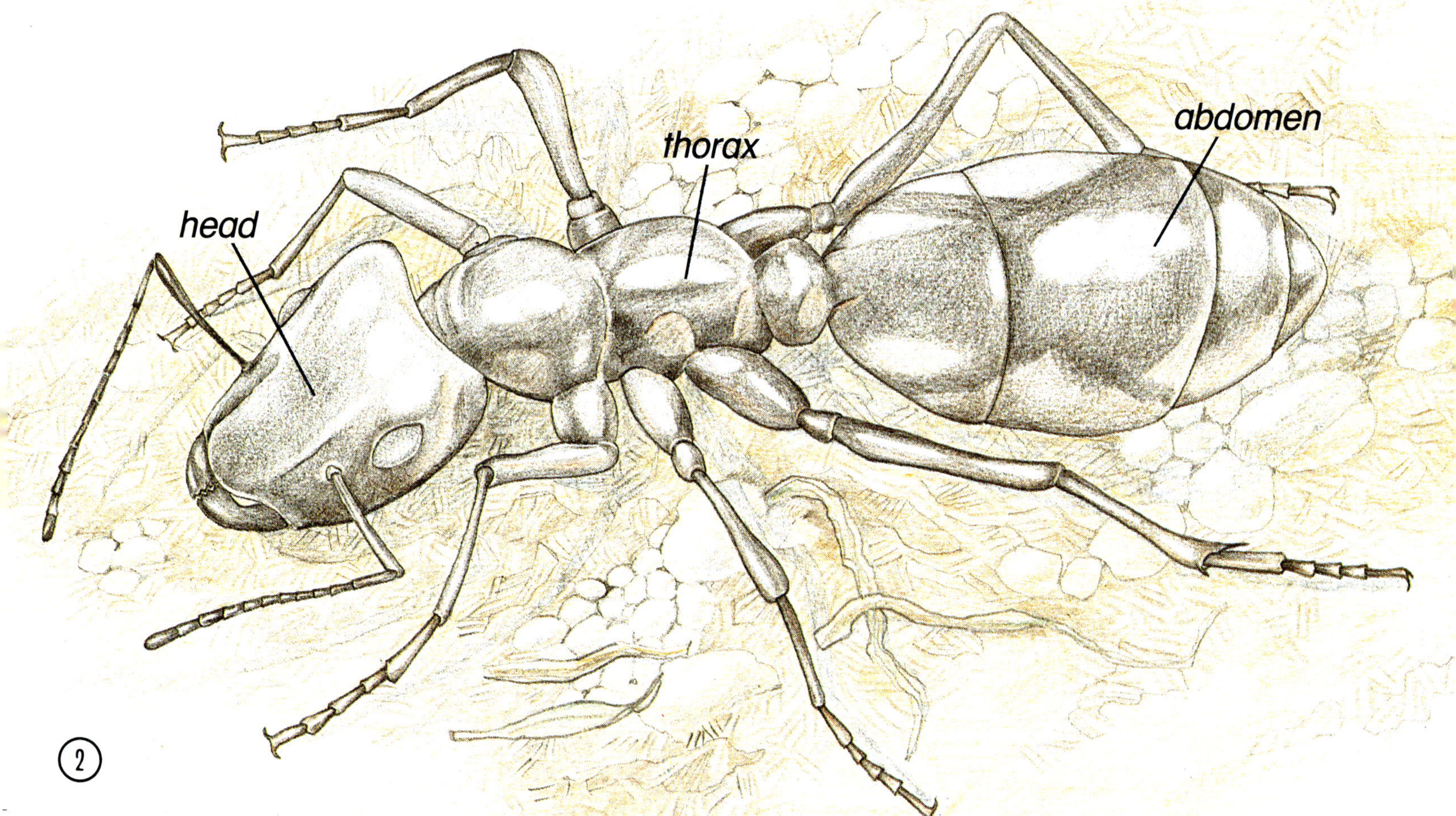

All insects
have six legs.

The legs
are joined
to the thorax.

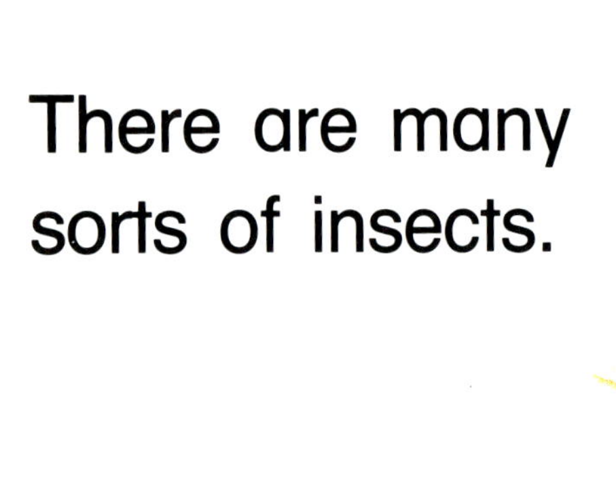

There are many sorts of insects.

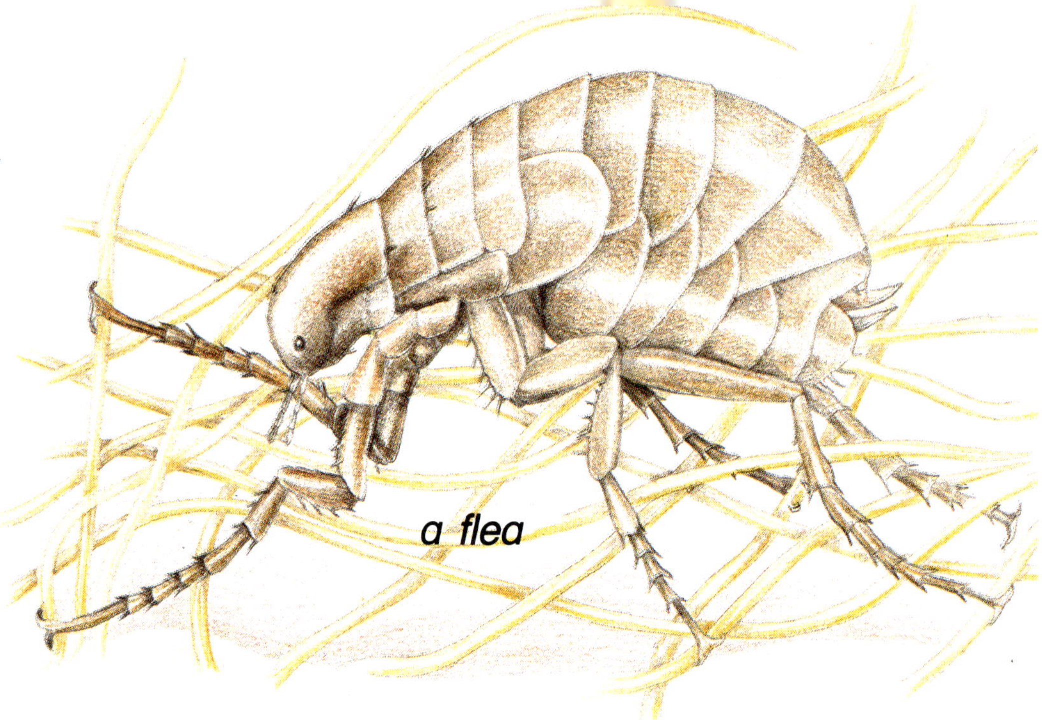

Some have no wings.

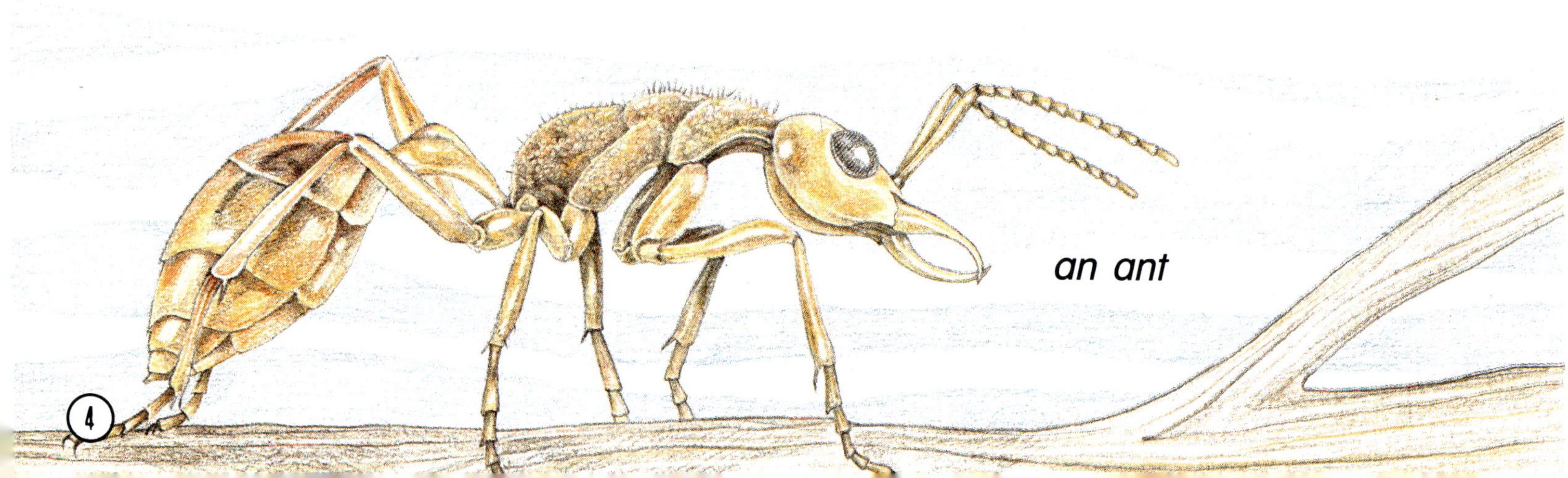

a flea

an ant

Some have two wings.

Some have four wings.

The wings are joined to the thorax.

An insect
has feelers
that stick out
of its head.

It's through
these feelers
that an insect
hears things,
or smells things,
or both.

An insect's eyes
can see
all around.

An insect
takes in air
through holes
in its abdomen.

An insect
has no backbone.
Instead, it has
a hard covering
on its body
called an exoskeleton.

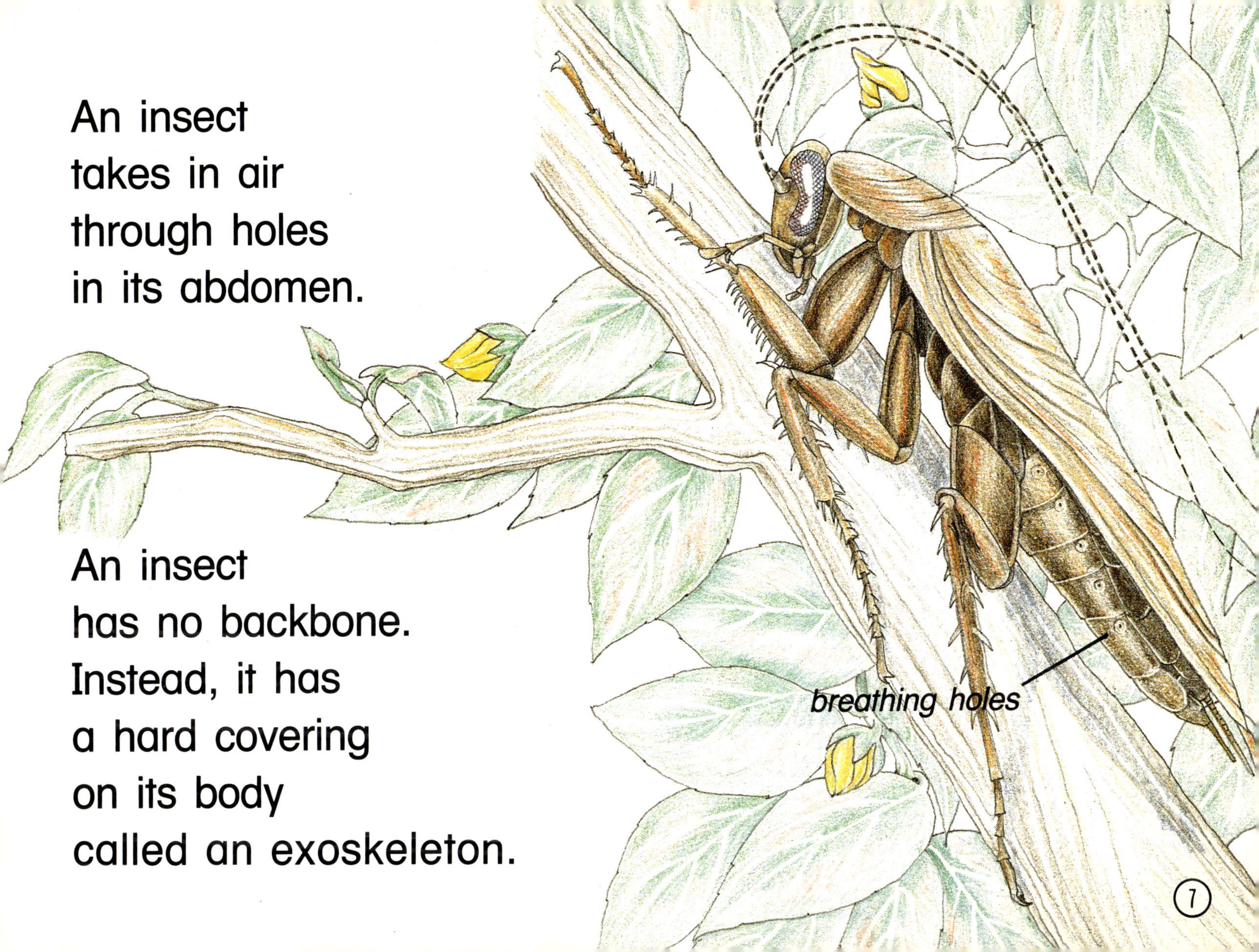

All insects lay eggs.
A butterfly comes from an egg.

The female Monarch butterfly
lays her eggs under a leaf.

The eggs grow
into caterpillars.

The fully grown caterpillar hangs by its tail end and sheds its skin. It becomes a chrysalis.

Inside its hard, green cover, the chrysalis changes. . . and hatches as a butterfly three weeks later.

Some insects
are useful to us.

Bees make honey.

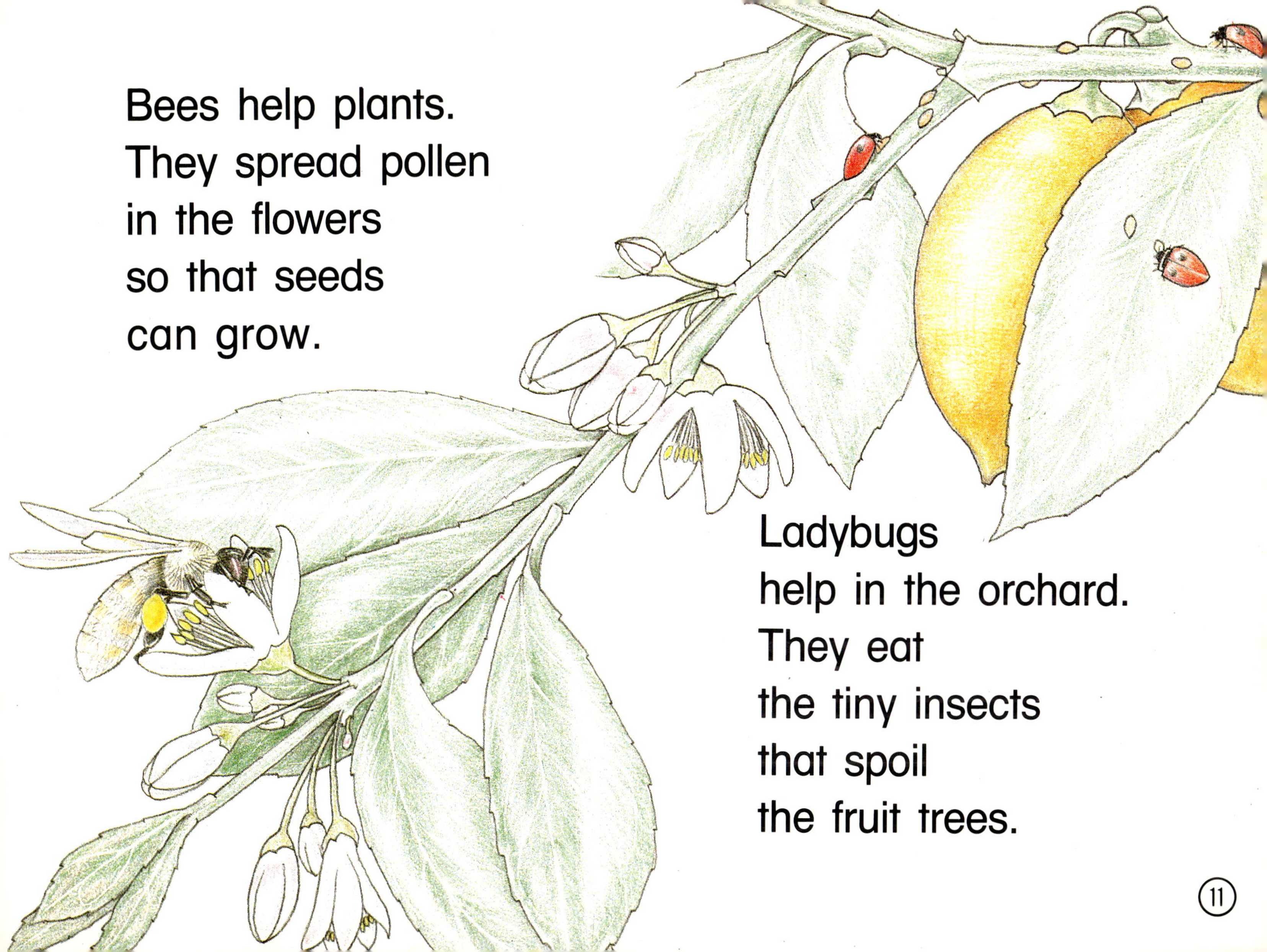

Bees help plants.
They spread pollen
in the flowers
so that seeds
can grow.

Ladybugs
help in the orchard.
They eat
the tiny insects
that spoil
the fruit trees.

Some insects are **not** useful to us.

Are fleas useful to us?

Are mosquitos useful to us?

Are flies
useful to us?

Are locusts
useful to us?

QUIZ

Ask your friend these questions.

Is a  an insect?

Is a an insect?

How many legs do insects have?

How do insects take in air?

How do some insects hear sound?

Name an insect that is useful to us.

Name an insect that is **not** useful to us.

Try these activities:

1. With a friend, do a survey about insects. Ask several people to name two or more insects that help humans. Write down each person's answers. After, see which insects were named most often. Talk about why people think well of those insects.

2. Work with four other students to put on a play about the life of a butterfly. Decide who will be the egg, caterpillar, chrysalis, butterfly, and narrator. Together write a script which tells about the stages in a butterfly's life. Perform your play for the class.